Level
# 2

# The Nature Kid's Guide to
# LLAMAS

# DAVID ANDERSON

LP Media Inc. Publishing
Text copyright © 2026 by LP Media Inc.
All rights reserved.



For information address LP Media Inc. Publishing,
30012 Variolite St NW, Princeton MN 55371
www.lpmedia.org

Publication Data

Llamas
The Nature Kid's Guide to Llamas — First edition.

Summary: "Learn all about Llamas, the Nature Kid Way"
— Provided by publisher.

ISBN: 979-8-89818-182-6

[1. Llamas – Non-Fiction] I. Title.

Title: The Nature Kid's Guide to Llamas

# CONTENTS


Llama Land . . . . . . . . . . 4

Mountain Roots . . . . . . . 6

Tall Tales . . . . . . . . . . 8

Lovely Layers . . . . . . . . 10

Look Out . . . . . . . . . . 12

Llama Lineup . . . . . . . . 14

Munch Time . . . . . . . . . 16

Fluffy Fleece . . . . . . . . 18

Hum Along . . . . . . . . . 20

Day by Day . . . . . . . . . 22

Prancing Pals . . . . . . . . 24

Dust Baths . . . . . . . . . 26

Herd Life . . . . . . . . . . 28

Spring Babies . . . . . . . . 30

Cute Crias . . . . . . . . . . 32

Mama Knows . . . . . . . . 34

Guard Duty . . . . . . . . . 36

Best Buddies . . . . . . . . 38

# LLAMA LAND

A llama can learn its own name and come when you call — just like a dog!

**Clip-clop! A llama trots through the barn door into the sun.**

Have you ever met an animal that can learn its own name, spit at enemies, and carry a heavy pack up a steep mountain trail? Meet the llama — one of the most surprising animals on the planet!

Llamas have been working alongside people for over six thousand years. They helped the Inca build an entire empire high in the Andes mountains of South America. Today they live on farms all over the world, and they are still full of surprises.

This book is going to show you why llamas are so much more than just tall, fluffy farm animals. Get ready to meet one of nature's most entertaining creatures!

# MOUNTAIN ROOTS

**Whoosh! A wild guanaco leaps across the rocky mountain path.**

Llamas come from South America. Their wild cousins are called **guanacos**, and guanacos still roam the high Andes mountains today.

A long time ago, people tamed wild guanacos. Over time, these animals became the llamas we know.

The Inca people loved their llamas. They used them to carry heavy loads up steep trails. Without llamas, mountain life would have been much harder. These sturdy animals helped build an empire!

TALL TALES
FUN FACT!
A llama weighs about five times more than an average second grader!

**Swoosh! A llama lifts its long neck high above the tall fence.**

A grown llama stands about six feet tall, and most of that impressive height comes from its long, graceful neck. That puts them eye to eye with most adults!

Llamas weigh between 250 and 450 pounds — much more than they look under all that fluffy wool!

Their legs are long and surprisingly strong. Llamas can carry up to a third of their own body weight on a pack saddle, making them one of the hardest working animals on any farm.

# LOVELY LAYERS

**Swish! A llama flicks its ears and fluffs up its woolly coat.**

A llama's coat is soft and thick. It has two layers. The outer layer keeps rain and wind away, while the inner layer is fluffy and warm.

Llamas have long, curved ears shaped like bananas. A split upper lip helps them pick just the right leaves. Instead of hooves, they walk on soft pads with two toes each.

Under all that fluff, llamas have strong bones. Their body is big and sturdy. Their teeth even keep growing their whole life, so they never wear down!

# LOOK OUT

FUN FACT!
A llama can spot a hawk in the sky from much farther away than you can!

**Crack! A twig snaps and a llama swivels its ears toward the sound.**

Llamas have great eyesight. Big, round eyes sit on the sides of their head. This lets them see almost all the way around without turning.

Each ear can turn on its own! Llamas move their ears to find where a sound comes from. They can hear even soft noises from far away.

A strong nose helps them too. Llamas can sniff out water from far away. With such sharp senses, they are always on the lookout for danger.

There are over one hundred thousand llamas living in the United States — more than in any country outside South America!

## Whomp! A shaggy Suri llama shakes its long, curly coat.

Not all llamas look the same. Some have short, smooth wool. These are called classic llamas, and they are strong and lean.

Woolly llamas have thick, fluffy coats. Fur covers most of their body, even their legs. They look like big puffballs walking across the field!

Suri llamas are the rarest type. Their wool hangs down in long, silky locks. It looks like they wear a fancy mop on their back! Each type has its own special charm.

# MUNCH TIME

DID YOU KNOW?
A llama eats only about two percent of its body weight each day — horses need twice that much!

**Chomp! A llama rips up a mouthful of fresh green grass.**

Llamas are **herbivores**, which means they eat only plants. Grass is their main food, and they spend hours grazing in the field each day. But llamas are picky eaters! They carefully choose which plants to eat and leave the rest alone.

Farmers also give llamas hay when fresh grass is hard to find. Some llamas get a little grain as a treat.

Llamas chew their food twice. First they swallow it, then bring it back up and chew it again slowly. This is called chewing **cud**, and it helps them squeeze every bit of nutrition from tough plants.

# FLUFFY FLEECE

Llama wool comes in more than twenty natural shades — from white to black and every brown in between!

## Buzz! A llama stands still as the farmer clips its soft, thick wool.

Once a year, farmers shear their llamas. That means they cut off the wool. It does not hurt — it is just like getting a haircut!

Llama wool is very warm and soft. People spin it into yarn, then use it to knit hats, scarves, and sweaters. The wool is also lighter than sheep's wool.

One llama can give five to seven pounds of wool at a time. That is enough to make several warm, cozy sweaters!

# HUM ALONG

DID YOU KNOW?
Llamas sometimes spit when they are angry — but they aim at each other, not at people!

# Hmmm! A llama hums gently to its friend across the pen.

Llamas are big talkers — but not with words! They hum to each other all day long. A soft hum means a llama is happy or curious.

A mother llama hums to her baby often. The baby hums right back! Each llama has its own special hum, like a voice you can recognize.

If a llama is scared or angry, it makes an alarm call. It sounds like a loud, shaky scream. When the whole herd hears it, they all look around fast.

# DAY BY DAY

FUN FACT!
Llamas sleep only about four hours
each night — you probably sleep
more than twice that much!

**Yawn! A sleepy llama stretches in the soft morning light.**

Llamas wake up with the sun. They start the day by eating grass, and the whole herd grazes together in the cool morning air.

By midday, llamas like to rest. They sit down and fold their legs under their body. Some close their eyes for a quick nap in the shade.

As the sun goes down, llamas eat again. Then they settle in for the night. They sleep lying down, close to each other for warmth and safety.

# PRANCING PALS

## Thump! A young llama bounces across the field with joy.

Llamas walk, trot, and run. They move both legs on the same side at the same time. This gives them a smooth, rocking walk that looks almost like dancing.

Young llamas love to run and play. They dash around the field and kick up their heels. This joyful jumping is called **pronking**!

Llamas are steady on rough ground. They can walk on rocks and steep slopes with ease. Even on bumpy mountain paths, they barely stumble.

# DUST BATHS

Llamas pick one special spot in the field to use as a bathroom — the whole herd shares it!

**Poof! A llama drops down and rolls in a patch of dry dust.**

Llamas love to roll in dirt! They flop onto the ground and wriggle around. Dust flies everywhere. It may look silly, but it helps them stay healthy.

Rolling in dust keeps bugs away. It also soaks up extra oil in their wool. Clean wool keeps llamas cool and comfy all day long.

After a dust bath, llamas shake off and walk away. They may look dusty, but they feel great. A good roll is like a spa day for a llama!

# HERD LIFE

FUN FACT!
Male llamas wrestle by bumping chests and wrapping their long necks together!

## Bump! Two llamas stand side by side. They are best friends.

Llamas are herd animals. That means they like to live in groups. A lonely llama is a sad llama — they need friends!

Most herds have about five to ten llamas. One llama often takes charge and watches for danger. The rest follow its lead and trust its warnings.

Llamas in a herd are close like a family. They graze together, rest together, and walk together. Being in a group makes them feel safe and happy.

SPRING BABIES
FUN FACT!
Mother llamas almost never have twins — it is one baby at a time, every time!

**Thud! A brand-new baby llama drops softly onto the grass.**

Most baby llamas are born in spring or summer. The warm weather helps them grow strong. A mother llama carries her baby for about eleven months — almost a whole year!

Baby llamas are called **crias**. They are born during the day, almost always in the morning. This gives them sunlight and warmth right away.

A newborn cria weighs about twenty to thirty pounds. It has long, wobbly legs. Within an hour, it can stand up on its own and start exploring!

# CUTE CRIAS

DID YOU KNOW?
Crias grow so fast that they can gain about one pound every single day!

**Squeak! A tiny cria calls out and nuzzles close to its mom.**

Crias are soft and fuzzy from the start. They have big, dark eyes and floppy ears. Their legs look too long for their little body!

A cria starts to run and play within a day. It bounces around the field near its mother, chasing and leaping with the other young llamas.

Crias drink their mother's milk for about four to six months. Then they start to munch on grass like the grown-ups. Before long, they look just like mini versions of their parents!

# MAMA KNOWS

34

## Sniff! A mother llama nudges her baby with her soft, warm nose.

Mother llamas are gentle and caring. They stay close to their baby at all times. If something seems wrong, the mom stands guard right away.

A mother llama does not lick her baby like a cow does. Instead, she nuzzles it with her nose. She sniffs her cria to learn its special scent so she can always find it.

As crias grow, the mother shows them what to eat and where to go. She teaches them how to be part of the herd. Good mamas raise good llamas!

GUARD DUTY
DID YOU KNOW?
One guard llama can protect a whole flock of over a hundred sheep — all by itself!

**Stomp! A guard llama stamps its foot at a sneaky coyote.**

Some llamas have a big job. They guard sheep, goats, and chickens! Farmers put one llama in with the smaller animals, and the llama keeps watch all day.

If a fox or coyote comes close, the llama jumps into action. It stands tall, stares hard, and stomps its feet. Most sly hunters run away fast!

Guard llamas are brave and strong. They do not need to be taught this skill. Keeping others safe just comes to them naturally.

BEST BUDDIES
FUN FACT!
Llamas and alpacas are cousins — but alpacas are only half as big!
38

**Baa! A llama rests in a sunny field next to its sheep friends.**

Llamas get along well with almost every animal they meet. They share fields with sheep, goats, horses, and even ducks. Their calm nature helps other animals feel safe and relaxed.

That same gentle quality is why people bring llamas to visit schools, hospitals, and care homes. A visit from a friendly llama has a way of making even the worst day feel better.

Now you know what makes llamas so special. They are strong, smart, hardworking, and surprisingly kind. Once you meet one, you will never look at a farm the same way again!

# GLOSSARY

### cria
A baby llama.

### cud
Food that comes back up to be chewed a second time.

### pronking
To eat grass or plants in a field.

### guanaco
A wild South American animal that is the llama's ancestor.

### herbivore
An animal that eats only plants.